I Do Not Want To

DISCARD

DISCARD

Written by Kathy Schulz
Illustrated by Sanja Rešček

Children's Press®
A Division of Scholastic Inc.
New York • Toronto • London • Auckland • Sydney
Mexico City • New Delhi • Hong Kong
Danbury, Connecticut

To Amy, my little sister
—K.S.

For Marijan, with love
—S.R.

Reading Consultants

Linda Cornwell
Literacy Specialist

Katharine A. Kane
Education Consultant
(Retired, San Diego County Office of Education and San Diego State University)

Library of Congress Cataloging-in-Publication Data

Schulz, Kathy.
 I do not want to / written by Kathy Schulz ; illustrated by Sanja
Rešček.
     p. cm. — (A rookie reader)
Summary: An older brother explains all the things he hates to do,
although he does them to set a good example for his younger brother.
 ISBN 0-516-24403-5 (lib. bdg.)   0-516-27845-2 (pbk.)
 [1. Brothers–Fiction. 2. Role models–Fiction. 3. Stories in rhyme.]
I. Rešček, Sanja, ill. II. Title. III. Series.
 PZ8.3.S2974Iac 2003
 [E]–dc21

                            2003007118

CHILDREN'S PRESS, and A ROOKIE READER®, and associated logos are
trademarks and or registered trademarks of Scholastic Library Publishing.
SCHOLASTIC and associated logos are trademarks and or registered
trademarks of Scholastic Inc.
1 2 3 4 5 6 7 8 9 10 R 13 12 11 10 09 08 07 06 05 04

3

I do not want to take a bath,

4

5

or eat my peas,

or do my math.

I do not want to wash my hair,

or get dressed up,

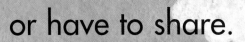

or have to share.

I do not want to sit up straight,

or take out trash,

or wash my plate.

21

I do not want to walk instead,

22

or wait my turn,

or go to bed.

I do not want to, but I do,

to show you what is good for you.

Word List (38 words)

a	good	out	turn
bath	hair	peas	up
bed	have	plate	wait
but	I	share	walk
do	instead	show	want
dressed	is	sit	wash
eat	math	straight	what
for	my	take	you
get	not	to	
go	or	trash	

About the Author

Kathy Schulz is an elementary school teacher and a big sister. *I Do Not Want To* was inspired by her own childhood memories and the stories she hears from her students. Kathy enjoys writing in rhyme and hopes to write many more stories in rhyme for young readers. She often thinks of ideas for her stories while she is sitting under a tree with Baxter, her 14-year-old dog.

About the Illustrator

Sanja Rešček is an illustrator of children's books, a designer, and a painter. She has been drawing since she was a little girl, mostly on the walls, but now she usually sticks to her paper. She has already illustrated over fifteen picture books and done a large number of illustrations for magazines, books, postcards, and stamps. She lives in Zagreb, Croatia.